information will make us transparent information will make us transparent

Published by Game Winner LLC

ISBN-13: 978-1977918451

ISBN-10: 197791845X

www.independentatmosphere.com

Smile

(while you stick the knife in)

PREFACE

It's not hard to see that something has gone horribly wrong with 'the American Dream'. Somewhere along the journey, we lost our way. This is evident in the way that we communicate information.

Information has always been sacred - but misinformation is diabolic and strategic. We are subjected to half-truths, misinformation and outright lies day in and day out from every imaginable source: our co-workers, our bosses, our leaders in the White House, our religious leaders, advertisements, the media, our friends and even our families.

Simply put, we live in a world where half-truths are born from fear, with a system that punishes the unlucky and allows the rich and privileged to live above the law.

There is enough documentation out there to make your head spin - detailing accounts of our system being manipulated to the benefit of rapists and killers, allowed to go free on technicalities. There are plenty of documented accounts of scandals, embezzlement and fraud.

With that being said, I'm not writing this book to cite magazines, websites and other authors - but to explore my frustration with injustice and social neglect.

Our system, processes, laws, representatives and leadership all enable the corruption that has infected every facet of our lives.

Instead of allowing for social and individual growth through a stable environment, we are caught in the crossfire of media scares, power struggles and games of financial gain.

It's frustrating to see a world focused on the symptom instead of the cause. A world where someone would purchase a patent on a technology that could improve the quality of life for millions of people, only to ensure that the patent would never see the light of day. Why would someone do such a thing? Because there would be negative financial impacts to certain 'interest groups'.

These are our realities.

After a while, these realities become poison... and this book is my attempt at expelling that poison in a creative way that inspires change and makes you thirst for information.

Information is out there - you just have to look for it.

Not all paths lead to enlightenment,
some lead to enjoyment
some lead to both.

Chapter 0

PRE-THOUGHTS

Patience.

A difficult practice when social prudence is void and even more imperative to captivate through change.

This is not to be confused with the majority sitting idly by, bathed in lies from our LCD television screens, watching the web of pre-meditated events play out. There is a vast difference between patient, complacent and ignorant.

Some take aggressive action, while others prey on the weak or less fortunate. This is the world we are living in – captivated by the fear they sell us and contently medicated because they tell us a pill will 'fix' our problems.

We have lost control of our society – as it was to be judged by the security and happiness of its citizens… How can you claim that we're a 'happy' nation when 1 in 4 adult women have some type of diagnosed mood disorder?

After a few repetitions of this cycle, the public begins to look like cash cows – bred for profit and slaughtered by process. I believe that we have more to offer than this comatose lifestyle we have embraced through the miracle

of pharmaceuticals – something of worth and meaning, whether in small doses (no pun intended) or on a larger scale (one we may not currently understand).

and now... let's take some drugs.

Chapter 1

DRUGS

You wake up early in the morning... so early that the sun isn't up yet but you can still see the gentle navy-blue glow from the horizon creeping playfully through gaps in your curtains.

Your head hurts with incredible pressure as pain emanates from the inside – a volcano stirring with nowhere to go. Every time your heart pumps you feel your head pound like a bass drum in a metal garage.

Getting up, you feel the icy floor under your bare feet, the chill running up your spine and distracting you momentarily from your pounding headache. With your second step towards the bathroom, your focus shifts magnetically back to the throbbing migraine-like pain.

You stumble a few more steps to your medicine cabinet, open it and rifle through with hopes to find encapsulated relief. Antacids, Anti-Diarrheals, Antibiotics (whoops, should have taken all of those – as directed), vitamins – ah here we go – pain relievers.

You attempt to open the child-proof bottle, which takes a couple tries in your half-awake state (damn child-proof caps).

Finally, you pour a cup of water and take some acetaminophen… Does that sound familiar?

Congratulations – you've taken drugs.

By definition, a drug is any substance that is absorbed into a living organism and alters its normal functions (physically or psychologically).

If you've ever taken something for a headache, upset stomach, sinuses – you've done drugs... However, if you've ever had any painkillers like Oxycodone or Morphine, then a special kudos to you, as you've basically had synthetic heroin.

Many drugs are synthetic forms of a naturally occurring chemical/compound or based on a naturally occurring chemical/compound. Take aspirin for example, where a chemical in willow tree bark is the basis of the synthetic active ingredient in aspirin. The same goes for morphine, heroin and oxycodone – all thanks to the poppy plant. Marinol is synthesized THC from Marijuana. When you can synthesize something that's naturally occurring, you can patent it and profit from it.

The word 'drugs' often has a negative connotation in the media or conversation. Listeners and viewers oftentimes hear the word 'drugs' and associate marijuana, cocaine, heroin or any other number of illegal narcotics – but is this negative connotation driven by the substances themselves?

Does the media not play a part in our Pavlov-like reaction to the word 'drugs'?

Nah...

Some people would lobby for a 'Drug Free America' while others lobby to 'Legalize the Plant'. Still others have an almost anarchist approach to legalize any-and-everything. So where do you begin to draw the line on a subject that affects us all? Drugs are an integral part of our life – no matter how you look at it, even for the people who tell you they've never done drugs... while taking a drag on their unfiltered cigarette and sipping their espresso.

CIGARETTES & COFFEE

Cigarettes can cause cancer – everyone knows this, yet people still indulge in this activity daily. The tobacco industry continues to profit, mostly thanks to nicotine and slick marketing, as the healthcare industry profits from the side effects of smoking – a win/win situation.

A question that the tobacco industry won't answer honestly is why they need all the different chemicals and additives in cigarettes... sure, they tell you it's for "flavor" or "burning consistency" but what it's really for is "side effects and residual revenue".

Take a look and see exactly what they're putting in your cigarettes:

- Cadmium
- Benzene
- Formaldehyde (embalming fluid)
- Nickel
- Ammonia
- Naphthalene (the ingredient in moth balls)

And that's just some of the 600 or so additives and ingredients in a cigarette --- which seems dwarfed by the 4,000 chemicals that you're inhaling once you actually light the cancerstick.

The combustion of those ingredients and additives with one another generates chemicals like carbon monoxide and hydrogen cyanide.

The common name for hydrogen cyanide was Prussic Acid and it was a main component of Zyklon B (Hitler's death gas in Concentration Camps) and is currently used in gas chambers by the US when a criminal is sentenced to death by gas... And this shit's going in your lungs when you smoke a cigarette?

Granted, some of these chemicals may appear to be relatively small doses but over time there's a cumulative

effect or buildup in your system – and with so many chemicals, it's a jackpot of possibility for cancer or complications down the road – a win for the tobacco industry and a win for the healthcare industry.

What's truly amazing is that the US Government has approved these chemicals for manufacturing in cigarettes as well as the public's consumption (seriously - WTF).

How about those fireproof cigarettes? Do you know how they're making them safer for you?

By applying ethylene vinyl acetate to your cigarette. Not familiar with that term? Hmmm how about we just call it a dab of glue, from a hot glue gun. Think I'm joking? Do your research.

Would you apply HMAs (Hot Melt Adhesive) to something you were about to smoke?

Now, smoking isn't free of long-term risks and we all know them by now, but why would you want to muddy the waters and add something like a synthetic hot glue compound to the mix of crap you're already inhaling?

And let's not mention the fact that tobacco companies can cut through red tape like a bulimic at a buffet line.

How is it possible that they can get away with putting anything they want in our cigarettes? Money talks.

They're in the process of banning Menthol cigarettes – but why? Why single out menthol over all the others? Don't they all cause cancer?

Some claim the flavor of menthol entices a younger smoking audience – as if the younger audience doesn't have the ability to choose for themselves or parents to help guide them and teach them (which they probably don't).

Why are we not putting the "choice" in the PUBLIC's hands (besides the fact that our government has bred us to be stupid...)?

They are inadvertently saying that we're incapable of making our own decisions… that we don't know what's best for ourselves. That's how it feels to me as these laws are being passed – it feels like an interest group is being protected or a long-range plan is being acted out as our freedoms are slowly and methodically being usurped in the name of safety, public health or national security.

If I want to kill myself with 2 packs of menthol cigarettes every hour on the hour, then that's my "God-given" right. I should be able to decide how MY life plays out (providing that it doesn't compromise another's) – that is an inalienable right – but it has been taken and raped by the judicial system's pimps, courtesy of the private sector's funding.

Time for some coffee...

COFFEE

What goes hand in hand with cigarettes? Coffee.

There's roughly 100 million people in the US who drink coffee every day, as compared to the 46 million that smoke cigarettes (many of the 46 million are also represented in the 100 million number, as a survey in 2008 showed that half of all smokers regularly drink coffee and smoke at the same time).

With a little quick math and a starting point of about 310 million US citizens, it looks like we're a nation full of drugees with +100 million people hooked on caffeine, doesn't it? (that's roughly 30%)

...and you said you didn't like drugs.

ALCOHOL

Around 2007 annual alcohol induced deaths were documented at around 20,000 – this number EXCLUDES accidents and homicides that were alcohol related. When you factor in the related accidents, the number lands somewhere around 85,000. So that's 65,000 alcohol related events... and we condone this.

That's 65,000 bar fights, battered spouses, raped daughters at college hazing parties, collisions with drivers minding their own business, and assorted other jackassery.

Yet there's absolutely nothing wrong with alcohol when you enjoy it responsibly.

A glass of wine, a scotch on the rocks, an ice cold beer on a hot summer afternoon… But if you decide to go drinking and driving then you're putting your life at risk along with any passengers in your vehicle and any people you pass headed to your destination.

Not a smart move.

Lucky for us, there are laws to govern what is an acceptable limit to drive and what isn't. But if you look at some reports out there, you'll notice that alcohol has rated as high as 3rd highest mortality rate in the US – right up there with Tobacco use (hmmmm?), poor diets / exercise habits, and stress.

Can you guess where marijuana rates on these lists? Can you guess how many deaths marijuana is directly responsible for? And I'm not talking about the idiots that go out there and smoke a joint and then drink a six-pack and try to drive… I mean DIRECTLY responsible.

It's a lot less than pharmaceuticals. It's a lot less than tobacco. It's a lot less than alcohol… but you already know this. I've never seen marijuana on these lists unless it's at the very bottom with a 0 beside it. Intriguing.

LOCO LOKO

There's all types of alcohol from moonshine to beer, wine, spirits - but recently there has been controversy over a certain alcoholic beverage called Four Loko. Some articles claim it contains as much alcohol as anywhere from 4-6 beers and 5 cups of coffee. Pretty bold statements by the media.

Most of us realize that the caffeine (and other additives) is what make the drink "unsafe" because people don't realize they're consuming so much alcohol due to seemingly lessened effects. If safety was the concern, why not sell it only in ABC stores to make it less accessible and to emphasize the strength of the product.

And to the argument that the effects of the caffeine make drivers more prone to drive – I'd be willing to bet that these same people who drive drunk on Four Loko would also drive after drinking a few beers or shots and would justify their actions by claiming they were being 'careful' or weren't feeling 'too drunk'.

What they don't realize is that their reaction time is slowed by a force beyond their control when they've been drinking. Oftentimes, victims in 'drinking and driving accidents' aren't even drinking – they're just innocent bystanders.

As painfully true as this is, some people still lack respect for alcohol.

Now, let's look at this think another way – our government is saying that we're incapable for deciding for ourselves what products to consume – and only what they deem 'safe' may we purchase.

Now I don't know about you, but I've got enough social responsibility not to go drinking and driving. Most people have the common sense not to do this, right? Of course, we all know that one idiot who claims he's fine to drive as he stumbles down the stairs with a beer bottle in his hand, which is why laws are there in the first place – to protect the many innocent from the few offenders.

But you've got to ask yourself at this point – do you really want to live in a society where the government – your ruling body – makes a decision, that in more or less terms specifies that the publics' discretionary abilities will be revoked by way of product banning (as opposed to informing)?

Shouldn't we put the responsibility where it belongs – on the governed body? If people continue to drink and drive put a heavier restriction on it – but when is enough 'enough' – restriction of driving for 5 years? 10 years? Hard labor? Death? How do we deem what "justice" is in regards to obeying the laws of social responsibility and social respect?

Switch gears for a moment and think about how Western medicine revolves around pills and surgery – when one takes a pill for something like a headache, we are simply masking the true root problem with a temporary cure.

There has to be SOME cause of the headache. The aspirin will mask the pain and make it go away – but something had to cause it.

Instead of investigating these causes, we have chosen, as a society, to be deceived… to be victims.

We're so eager to believe anything that 'seems to make sense' or appears neat and complete – and what makes more sense than physical proof? Such as the type of proof that's attained by the pharmaceutical industry – you are depressed – they give you a pill and the depression goes away – in your mind, it fixed the problem, but unfortunately it only fixed the symptom, not the problem.

Through the joys of marketing and *conditioning* we have

been led to accept this masking of the problem through symptom-only solutions.

In turn, I believe that we've been looking at the Menthol / Four Loko equations in the wrong light - for banning the products would simply be masking a symptom instead of fixing the true problem.

At the heart of this tobacco or alcohol-controversy, the real cause is lack of social responsibility. It could be argued there is a lack of social responsibility on both the governed body and more importantly, the governing body.

This has been omitted from most parenting and institutions (not all people are good parents – some are more like guardians and don't foster their child's development, some try to be friends and give no guidance).

We need to figure out how to implement social responsibility back into our society and learn some social respect for one another – if nothing more, so that we may live-on as an evolving, thinking collective.

Every day we blame the individuals – the results of the system – instead of identifying what is broken in the system that allowed the result and fixing this gap to ensure it does not continue in the future.

ALCOHOL VS. MARIJUANA

The fact that we haven't integrated the idea of social responsibility, transparency and social respect through our educational system or more importantly; that we haven't exhibited a "leadership by example" approach to teach our future generations the importance of these ideals, simply demonstrates how primitive our society is.

Let's kick this off with a fun fact – you can't overdose (OD) from marijuana. You can't say the same for alcohol… after enough consumption in a short enough period of time you'll have alcohol poisoning – and long term, possibly cirrhosis of the liver.

Granted, for marijuana *smokers* you might have some respiratory-related incident with extended use, but there are many other ways to use marijuana without combustion – such as ingestion or vaporization – both of which have ZERO long-term side effects (such as the side effects of smoking or drinking excessive alcohol). Makes you wonder which one should be illegal…

So why do we condone alcohol in our society and not marijuana (legally speaking)?

Well, the initial reason marijuana was looked down upon was a smear campaign around the 1930's. Then in the 70's it became ammo for Nixon to go after the hippies. The

question remains – why the hell we haven't legalized it by now?

We have the means to control it, regulate it, distribute it, benefit from it, tax it and profit from it – why are we not taking advantage of this revenue generator?

Why are we wasting resources prosecuting people for possession of marijuana, paraphernalia, etc – why are we wasting resources, tax dollars, jail and prison space on these people?

Keeping someone in prison costs about $40-50 a day or around 14-19k a year – and we've already got between 2-3 million people locked up as it is… That's about 1 in every 100 US citizens are behind bars. And the US is doing nothing but adding more prisons and more laws to continue the downward spiral.

LD50 & MARIJUANA : DOES NOT COMPUTE

As previously stated, there is no practical way to die or fatally overdose from Marijuana. This is based on the LD50 - a quantitative way to state the toxicity of chemicals, where 50% of the lab rats die with a particular dosage.

Lethal Dosage 50% - LD50.

This idea came about in the late 1920's by J.W. Trevan - the idea of using death as a baseline of comparison.

It would be impossible to consume the amount of marijuana you would need to overdose and die, which is roughly 40,000 times the amount it takes to get you high.

40,000x

Think of it this way - if just one hit got you high, you'd need 40,000 to die - within about 15 minutes.

15 minutes

Alcohol on the other hand only requires about 5 – 10 times the amount it takes to get you intoxicated to be fatal.

5x - 10x

...and which one's safer? ...and which one's legal...

So let's assume it takes about 4 shots in 15 minutes to get you blitzed, then 20-40 shots in 15 minutes would kill you (assuming the 5-10x rule of alcohol).

But let's say you can really hold your liquor (full-blown or partially-blown alcoholic) and it takes about 10 shots in 15 minutes to get you wrecked, then it would take 50-100 shots in 15 minutes to kill you.

When the coroners got there, they could sell your blood back to the ABC store.

Marijuana has obviously not been illegalized because it's a danger toxically - the reasons are simply political.

MARIJUANA

In 2009 there were about 850,000 people arrested for cannabis related crimes in the US and approximately $42 billion dollars spent on the war against marijuana ALONE.

WTF.

To put that in quick perspective - we could save that 42 billion and convert it into 560,000 jobs paying an annual salary of $75k/each.

Since hundreds upon thousands of books are already
written about marijuana and most of you already know a
good deal about it through TV documentaries,
reading or first-hand experience – I'll just highlight a
couple more areas of interest and a few numbers.

Only a few people still believe that marijuana is illegal
because it's bad for you – most of us know it was initially a
smear campaign designed to protect the timber industry,
as we've seen the numerous products that can be made out
of hemp such as paper, rope, oils and dermatological
products.

If you're not familiar with Anslinger (the first Federal
Bureau of Narcotics Drug Czar) then you owe it to
yourself to do an internet search on him and his racist
remarks on marijuana usage – he's a charming character
with such quotes as…

"You smoke a joint and you're
                likely to **kill** your brother."

"The most **violence**-causing drug
                in the history of mankind."

"Reefer makes darkies think
                they're as good as white men."

"There are 100,000 total marijuana smokers in
the US, and most are Negroes, Hispanics,
Filipinos and entertainers.
Their Satanic music, jazz and swing, result
from marijuana usage.
This marijuana causes white women to seek
sexual relations with Negroes,
entertainers and any others."

Wow.

This guy's a class act.

After the reefer madness infected the nation, it was
followed up by a war on the hippies deemed "The War On
Drugs" by President Tricky-Dick Nixon when large
amounts of money were injected into a new governmental
body (dubbed the DEA) through Nixon's Reorganization
Plan #2 in 1973.

During 1973, the budget for the DEA was roughly $75
million – it's grown 34x since then (coming in around $2.6
billion in 2009).

How about the positive effects of cannabis? We've all
heard how you can make paper from it and rope or how

you can use the oil… but how about the experiments with injecting THC directly into a tumor? How about the receptors in your brain designed for cannabinoids (THC)?

Maybe it's about time society gave this plant a chance – medically, industrially and recreationally speaking.

THE REST OF 'EM

Getting "high"…

Most people "get high" every single day and don't even know it. You do it either when you first wake up, or when you first get to work. It's a morning ritual for you.

Every morning it's the same process – take the substance and put it in the white filter paper. Get your water ready.

Add your additional substances (synthetic or natural additives?)… and finally, you enjoy your cup of coffee – with all the caffeinated bliss it brings as it gets you "high" for somewhere between 30 minutes and 2 hours.

Just because it doesn't make you hallucinate doesn't mean you're not getting high with caffeine – it's just condoned by society because it's used responsibly (you don't see coffee drinkers popping 10 caffeine pills at the same time they're drinking a large cup of coffee do you?

My position on drugs is multi-faceted, as I can see the necessity to legalize them all and the benefits they can bring to certain individuals and circumstances. I can also see potential misusage – such as driving while using – but is this not the same as drinking and driving? It all goes back to responsibility.

To exemplify the benefits – I can see ecstasy usage for soldiers back from war or for individuals needing calming therapy sessions and to feel more empathetic towards their loved ones, possibility rehabilitative situations for the abused.

Besides the health-system needs, I can see marijuana usage for the everyman when he needs to relax and unwind. I can see mushrooms for the thinker who wishes to explore his or her mind.

The key is responsible usage. I believe we can set the stage for responsible usage as we lead by example with future generations.

Speaking of leading by example, I believe Portugal is on the right track – legalizing everything.

Crazy, right?

Their philosophy is that they would rather offer treatment, focus on prevention and help those that want

help instead of driving people further and further into isolation. (*treat the cause not the symptom*)

Within 5 years of Portugal legalizing all street drugs in 2001, street overdoses dropped nearly 30% and HIV infections from dirty needles dropped about 72% --- think of all the lives this could save...

I would much rather someone of legal age to be able to go to a store and buy cocaine, heroin or ecstasy instead of risking a shady deal with someone they barely know just because they wanted to 'try it'.

To further explore this example of a potentially shady deal, the first-time buyer would not understand what the substance is about to do, what to expect, how much of a dosage they are taking (or can take without extreme side effects/fatality), the purity of the substance, the security of the meeting location and a plethora of other variables.

By eliminating this aspect of 'drug-dealing' through regulation, it will free up the police for the important tasks - like investigations and protecting the public from the real 'bad guys' – rapists, murderers, thieves… not the guy taking some X with his girlfriend over the weekend or the middle-aged business men sharing a joint after work – those aren't the enemies, they're our neighbors, friends and family.

As we reform the system, we need to be conscious of life

experiences – you only get to live once. If you want to do something in your life, you should have the legal ability to do it (as long as it doesn't compromise another's life).

Who do they think they are telling us that we can't responsibly take peyote, mushrooms or salvia?

I'm not saying to turn the country into a drug-crazed mob. Instead, I'm proposing that there's room for everyone's lifestyle, with the understanding that *people will find a way to gain the experiences they seek.*

If we truly wanted to make society "safer" in regards to drugs, we would focus on the cause and not the symptoms. In turn, we would legalize them to ensure consistency, proper dosage, warnings and precautions, security and sanity - and we would offer help to those that needed it.

Pull back from the thoughts of morality and legalization and imagine a future where specific "drug" courses are taught - but not like any in a school right now.

How about one where you actually took the drug during class for some "hands on" experience? Think about how your respect for a substance would change if you could take it in a controlled environment (dosage, purity, information, guide, etc all controlled).

I'm sure marijuana lovers can imagine a course on

marijuana: historical background, real world scenarios of industrial, manufacturing and healthcare industry usage.

Horticultural training – including cross-breeding (and genetic modification in the not too distant future), and the parts of the course that everyone would be looking forward to – the application section: a joint, blunt, bowl, bong, steamroller, bubbler, vaporizer and edibles (brownies/cookies/cannacracker) – trying each way mentioned to experience the different delivery methods.

Not to mention the introduction to different grades (schwag, mids, heady, chronic/exotic) – most often staying with a bassline strain for the majority of the course and only straying to exemplify a point (showing the diversity of the strains - one makes you sleepy, one gives you a body buzz, one gives you energy, etc).

Or how about a later course where you explored consciousness through the usage of Amanita mushrooms (the red ones with white dots on them, like the ones a certain plumber ate to grow big) as well as the usage of Psilocybin mushrooms (the typical "magic mushrooms" people think of when they hear the word "trippin").

Pure DMT? Possibly even sensory deprivation tanks?

Most of the problems encountered within 'drug usage' is based on one of the following factors; environment, mindset, dosage, interaction.

A person's environment is critical when taking drugs (especially for the first time – don't be superman and take your first dose of mushrooms in a crowded mall with your idiot friends – have some social responsibility).

Often many people are already on one medication and fail to think about how a drug can interact with another drug – this is commonplace when you hear about OD's in the paper regarding sleep aids, pain killers and alcohol in combination…

Dosage includes purity of substance while interaction contains implications of both environmental interactions (you + busy street = ER visit) as well as internal interactions (MAOI's involved? Alcohol? Etc).

For some, this is all a recreational end-goal – for others it can be spiritual enlightenment – a religious experience.

WHAT'S THE USE?

Within the typical context of society, drugs have a negative connotation. When you hear "drugs" you don't think about acetaminophen – you think about crack cocaine and meth - or a pothead so burned out that s/he can't maintain a steady job or support his/her family.

A typical view of drugs is that they are an escape method - a way to escape the pain in your life or something you don't want to deal with. But how about the other reasons people might use drugs?

To calm their nerves and allow them to cure their restless night, for the desire to eat when going through treatments as a cancer patient, or maybe to reflect on their day or a situation…

How about the inner connection a user might get when meditating on mushrooms or marijuana, just as shamans have for hundreds and thousands of years? To see inside oneself in a different light perhaps?

Past cultures not only condoned this ritualistic usage but condoned the shaman being stones practically 24/7 – what an intense job that must have been.

The shaman was often the seer of the tribe, guiding spiritual development of its members as well as supposedly influencing the outcome of crops, weather, good fortune and more.

The irony of the drug situation in America is this: people are going to do what they want – the law is just getting in the way and deterring a few people.

If you want to try cocaine, you're going to find someone

who knows someone and you're going to get it – it's as easy as that.

If we legalize all drugs, we can moderate the dosage so people know what they're getting and know how much to take to stay "safe" (according to LD50's). They will know the purity of the substance and have all of this information from a credible, and more importantly, a safe source and safe location.

When you remove the taboo, you remove the allure

I'm sure this doesn't apply to everyone - for some will embrace the culture wholeheartedly, reliving the 70's, complete with bell-bottoms and hair in places it shouldn't be.

$50,000,000,000.00 SAVINGS!!!!

The war on drugs has been over for a long time – in fact, it was a war that could never truly be "won" (almost like Vietnam).

We're talking about 50 BILLION dollars in spending between Federal and State agencies, focused on drug prevention – as we saw, 42 of that is focused specifically on marijuana.

Let's pose a hypothetical situation - we've been fighting this war on drugs so long, we're not sure what to do with the drugs or the funding - what do we do?

Starting with the 50 billion spent on drugs, we cut 42 right off the bat (the marijuana portion), put it to GOOD use (public benefit) then take the other 8 and target something that does no one any good – rape, child porn, etc.

Next, we release the imprisoned that were locked up for minor drug charges (murder related? Sorry ☹ do not pass go, do not collect 200 dollars - you've got to stay).

We start selling drugs where they need to be sold (create a distribution method like ABC stores that are regulated and licensed).

Then we test the purity of substances and create non-invasive systems and processes for users to get information or get help when necessary.

If the government taxed all drugs in this manner – they could generate revenue that could actually be used for things that we need like guns! Guns, bombs, and biological weapons!

I'm only joking of course – what we need are things like more teachers (and better pay for them)...
...or we could use the money for fixing some of the shittiest

gridlocks around our nation and building new roads, highways and bridges (time is money – let's not spend it sitting in traffic – and besides, chances are likely that your 500k is ticking as you'll see…) – God forbid we spent some on the realistic replacement of internal combustion engines and move towards 'green' vehicles…

…or how about general investing in our future, as a society? As a species?

Back to the topic at hand, please don't think that my position on the legalization of drugs in America condones the cartels invading across the lines of the Mexican border with their drugs, guns and violence or the flourishing of gangs that surge with drug control/distribution in their area.

I believe funding should remain to combat cartels, local/global gangs – thereby reducing illegal international activity to a local matter, by way of legalization (no need to smuggle it in if you can get more/better for cheaper right down the street).

Hopefully other countries will adopt the same thinking started by Portugal and break down their laws against drugs as well, offering help to users that need it instead of instilling fear… or worse, without regulation, the inexperienced user's chance of overdose on harder substances increases because of misinformation about the substance or proper dosage.

CONSPIRACY?

Let's think about the "Drug War" in another way. What if the "Drug War" was a good thing? Not only a good thing, how about a profitable necessary evil?

Is it possible that the people who truly control America profit from the war on drugs (like they profit from war in general)?

Every time a law enforcement officer is issued gear, our tax dollars pay and someone profits.

Not to mention that the tax dollars that the drug dealer pays when they spend their drug money on some new merchandise - essentially/theoretically pays the officer's salary.

FUN WITH NUMBERS

Taking data from the DEA's reported seizures in 2009, let's run some numbers and see how much sales tax (government profit) would have been generated if the drugs had been sold...

- 49,000 kgs of cocaine
- 640 kgs of heroin
- 666,000 kgs of marijuan
- 1,700 kgs of methamphetamine
- 2,950,000 doses of hallucinogens

Almost everyone has seen drugs circulated at one point or another – either through a transaction or recreation – you know they are plentiful.

Chances are - if you've ever been 'holding' then you know that the numbers above don't represent half of what's out there in the streets and available to the public with the right connection.

My point here is that what they have seized is just a tip of the iceberg and they know it…

Take a look at the math and you'll see how "profitable" the drug war can be (besides all the money made off the gadgets and gizmos purchased for drug enforcement personnel - from the gun on their hip to the GPS in their car to the stapler on their desk - someone is profiting).

Let's run some numbers based on internet blogs and stats (keep in mind, these numbers are assuming "street level" consumer costs - not distribution costs):

Cocaine is estimated anywhere from $30-60 for a gram. (note - a kilogram (kg) is 1000 grams). Assuming we take the medium of 45$ a gram we could assume the street value of a kg of cocaine is about $45,000.

The average sales tax across the US is about 5.5% of every dollar – which would generate about $2,475 of tax from a kilogram (kg) of cocaine (for simplicity sake, we'll call it $2,500).

Follow me here… we're on a mission to figure out how much sales tax the amount of drugs seized would potentially net…

So with 49,000 kg's sold, and at $2,500 of sales tax from every kg, the cocaine seized would theoretically generate $122,500,000 in sales tax – One Hundred and Twenty Two… million dollars.

Heroin numbers are a little more rough – internet values per gram ranging around $125-180, I'm sure it can range higher or lower depending on purity and location.

Assuming $150 a gram, that's $150,000 per kg and roughly $8,000 generated in sales tax per kg. Remember, there were 640 kgs seized so that's $5,120,000 theoretically generated in sales tax for heroin seized.

Websites and blogs detail prices for marijuana with

'schwag' going for about 10$ a gram, 'mids' for $15 a gram, chronic/heady/exotic for $20-30 a gram.

Let's assume $15 a gram on average, totaling $15,000 per kg (sold at street level) – and 666,000 kgs were seized – which would have generated nearly $550,000,000 in sales tax.

Holy shit.

That's nearly half a billion sales tax dollars (potentially) just from the numbers with marijuana and just from the amount that the DEA reported seizing.

Let's stop right there, we won't even estimate hallucinogens (which was estimated around 20$ a hit yielding approx 3.2 million in sales tax).

Remember, the potential sales tax generated from the seized marijuana alone @ ~$550 million was at 5.5%... you could exponentially increase that number with proper taxation (10-30%) divided between the seller and the purchaser).

What the government makes on the sales-tax side of the equation above is minuscule in comparison to the potential earnings that could be brought to the table if taxation AND regulation of substances were both put into effect.

When you look at all the responsible buyers throughout

the US that would love to purchase at a legal dispensary knowing quality and quantity of product is exactly what is advertised as, in a safe environment without fear of persecution or conviction - for relief and medical needs.

PS – taxes @ 20% = about 2 billion in pure profit

FEAR OF CHANGE

One fear of a drug-friendly America (or at the minimum – a Pot-friendly America) might be that $42 billion dollars worth of jobs just went out the window…

Sure, job needs may change, but that doesn't mean the government people have to – they should have the option to be redeployed.

Realistically, think about all of the jobs that would be created with marijuana alone – the growers, the dispensaries, the accessories, the gadgets, the culture, the updated coffee houses – the regulators, federal inspectors and the researchers needed to explore what could be used medicinally to enhance the quality of life for people less fortunate.

When I say "regulators and federal inspectors" I'm talking about inspectors that are FOR the people and have "the peoples" best interests in mind – not someone getting

kickbacks from riders on bills or someone working for Big Tobacco.

Video killed the radio star - Corporations kill a product's soul.

The 'root problem' with America definitely isn't illegal drugs...

THE FDA

While we're on the topic of drugs, let's take a brief look at the FDA - The Food and Drug Administration.

Why would we combine food AND drug administration together? That seems a little odd to me.

More-so than odd, that almost sounds like insider trading to some degree – being that you've got the power to deem a food additive or ingredient is "safe" (aspartame? Olestra? MSG? etc.) ... and you've also got stock in the decisions of which drugs get approved for treating the "side effects" caused (by a strange coincidence) previously approved drugs – simply amazing.

Pharmaceutical drugs are man-made. When something is "man-made", it can be patented. That's where you can start profiting from it.

The fact that you can't patent a natural cure is a main reason that they aren't condoned by Western medicine and instead the "treatments" are surgery or drugs, pick your poison.

I'm not saying that everything can be cured by natural remedies (maybe it can, maybe it can't) – the point of this discussion is that if it works (truly works) it should be condoned simply for the benefit of someone enhancing their quality of life (and perhaps quantity of life as well) – as opposed to a *profit-focused* mentality.

I believe that the FDA does some good out there as well – protecting the public from ill goods that would make us sick.

But I also believe that the FDA has a vein of greed surging through it – redirecting its moral compass on certain decisions here and there. Knowing that products will slowly deteriorate some of the governed body's health (depopulation?) and benefiting financially on their lackluster hope of recovery through treatment after treatment.

Hundreds of billions of dollars are spent on the "treatments" for cancer, either through direct or indirect costs, it's still a billion-dollar business... it just varies at how MANY billions...

What if all this money could be saved by a natural cure or a simple one time pill or one time treatment?

A true cure, without treatments.

But since there's no money in a cure (and greed and power are rampant) – I guess we're all at the mercy of the almighty dollar.

If you haven't done your research on the FDA I strongly urge you to take a look at their decision making skills and reasoning, then ask yourself if this is the governing body we want protecting us…

Sure, I agree we need regulators ensuring the quality of

the food we consume or additives put in our food – but I also believe that information should be free and decisions should not be swayed by money.

If there's a cancer-causing additive or other residual effect from that additive, it should be marked unsafe and require a warning label (like the ones the cigarette cartons contain) so that the buyer is aware that it contains harmful chemicals and can make a more informed decision whether to consume/use that product or not.

BIG PHARMA VS DRUGS

Let's take a look at some of the numbers for Big Pharma:

- *US Prescription sales = $290 Billion dollars (2008)*

- *Approximately 27 million people (almost 10% of the population) are on antidepressants in the US (2009)*

- *The anti-depressant market is about $11 billion market in the US (2010)*

With just a few rough numbers to know what we're talking about, you can easily see that Big Pharma is a huge industry and a force to be reckoned with (money talks).

The illegal drug trade market was valued at around $320 billion (around 2008) – but this was a global number… and we're spending $290 billion on prescription sales, just in the US!?

Hmmm… we're starting to look even more like junkies...

The breakdown on the $320 billion global drug market shows a landslide market for cannabis around $140 billion, a close second by cocaine at around $70 billion and opiates

(opium poppy = morphine, codeine) closing third place around $65 billion.

That's $275 billion just on those 3 substances (technically 2 substances and 1 category).

VICTIMIZE ME

They say currently that about 5-9% of Americans are depressed?

Seriously?

Some people are in 3rd World Nations and don't have any food or shelter – and we complain that we're 'sad' because we can't find love?

We complain about our anxiety due to a weekly meeting, or that our "to-do" list is too long, and how we can't get to sleep or manage to steady our nerves throughout the day… unless we can take our colorful capsulated friend.

*We have become addicts to pills that cure our symptoms
but leave the cause to fester.*

*We fall victim to the system - a system of waste.
Systematic waste.*

There's been a lot of numbers thrown around – millions… billions… there was the $42 billion or so spent on the marijuana war – let's break that down. 42 billion. How much loot is that?

We'll start small (ha) with one billion $1,000,000,000

You could buy

- 16 million video games – brand new (60/ea)
- 2 million 36-42" flat screen LCD HDTVs
- 1.8 million laptops ($550/ea)
- 6,666 houses (assuming 150k/house)
- 20,000 salaries @ 50k/ea
- 40,000 electric cars (assuming 25k/car)

So that's what a billion dollars could buy you in rough terms.

Time to amp these numbers up and work with the $42 billion spent solely on the war against pot.

Now, instead of 16 million brand new video games, how about we buy some brand new shoes for people who can't afford them?

With $42 billion to work with, we'd have something to the tune of 672 million brand new pairs of shoes @ $60 each.

But wait a second – the population of the US is only about 310 million… that means that every person in the US would have roughly $120 year to spend from the government on new shoes.

EVERY person.

And that's just if we stop the war on pot and redirected our focus to legalization – not to mention the revenue generated from legalization and regulation.

For the person reading this that might be saying "why would every person need $120 for new shoes from the government?" - open your mind… I'm only putting these thoughts into perspective in an attempt to give you a different view to see things from.

It's not the point that every man, woman and child gets $120 for shoes – it could be $120 for gas, groceries, porn…

The point is that it's enough money that everyone could be affected - and if we can reach all these people with this type of budget, imagine how many TRULY needy people would benefit - driving their quality of life higher.

Back to the 42 billion dollar breakdown - 40,000 electric cars turns into a little over 1.6 million electric cars for the US citizens – not enough for everyone, but it's a start.

6,666 houses turn into about 280,000 houses for the homeless.
1.8 million laptops are now 76 million laptops.

To put that in perspective, there are about 75 million children in the US (2009/2010) – about 25 million of each fall into following age ranges 0-5, 6-11, 12-17.

So with 76 million laptops, we could ensure that every child in the US gets exposure to the technology and access to it, as well as fostering their development for tomorrow with the tools of today.

NEW PERSPECTIVES

Certain people in society may not see the necessity some claim for altered mind-states just as certain people may not see the necessity for going to church.

Just because we cannot see the other person's inner benefits or contentment doesn't mean it's less valued than our own.

Society has forgotten this and in turn, ostracized the "strange" for their wicked ways or cast judgment upon them by the masses.

In the US, if you're Muslim - you're a bomber.
If you're Jewish - you're wealthy.
If you're a Christian - you're "in".

This is a solid mentality for most of the cash cows out there.

Most of our 310 million citizens probably believe the lines above and regularly make these associations.

Perception is reality and when your head is up your ass, you're blind.

Welcome to America.

Chapter 2

WELCOME TO AMERICA

"History is a myth men agree to believe." – Napoleon

Revisionist history is the act of revising historical facts to support an agenda – and it's still happening all around you. Many people are unaware they've been lied to their entire life by sources they deemed credible (schools, governments, religious leaders).

The system is broken on every level and continues to deteriorate as information is withheld or skewed for self-serving reasons (just like the smear campaign for marijuana - all for the self-serving profit of the timber industry).

It's ironic that hundreds of years ago, the settlers left England for religious freedom (among other reasons, but this was a key one) – and here were are in 2011, still searching for our unalienable rights as they are dissolved in the name of national security.

Unfortunately there are no more 'far away lands' to escape to, and we will soon be forced to deal with the injustices and cyclical corruption or face a dismal outcome.

Why does our society continue to perpetuate the lies from the past?

In school we all learned that people in Christopher Columbus' times and earlier believed the world was flat - although, since about 400 BC, people have known the world to be round… how strange.

Many say American Settlers were heroes? Some were – but I thought many were sadistic murderers who stole land from the Native American Indians and then gave them blankets with disease. Then again the Spaniards decimated many native people on their voyages as well, so this systematic cultural destruction appears to be a recurring theme in our socio-economic evolution.

In 1775, Paul Revere made a brave ride… but only for about 12 miles. Israel Bissel made an even more incredible ride - but was hardly even mentioned throughout history (and never had a poem written in his honor – such as The Midnight Ride of Paul Revere).

Israel Bissel – a 23 year old postal worker who rode about 350 miles from Boston to Rhode Island, Connecticut, New York, New Jersey and finally ended in Philadelphia. You tell me who the real "hero" is…

The only reason we know about Paul Revere is because a popular writer (Henry Wadsworth Longfellow) at the time wrote about him – because his name was easier to rhyme to.

Throughout history, we (humans) have revised, rewritten, manifested, omitted, silenced and forgotten more truths than is possible to imagine.

We have done this in efforts to retain power – knowledge is raw power.

Let's take a look at some examples of control mechanisms that have been used in the US. The next few sections are only a small sample of the ways we have been controlled (or conditioned to be controlled) – but the conditioned behaviors do not have to continue within our society.

As we identify the stimuli and response correlation between control mechanisms and their influence upon us, we can change external control to self-control.

WILLIE

There was a man who wrote a paper on slavery back in the 1700's – how to control slaves and keep control for generations to come.

Quite sadistic, but I urge you to read it to become educated on the psychological tactics that people in control have been implementing for years on the public – the Willie Lynch letter (or Willie Lynch Paper).

Willie was a British slave owner from the West Indies – it's said that the term "lynching" was derived from his name, and as evil as this bastard was, he was smart.

His paper claimed to keep slaves for +300 years – multiple generations in the future – but what was his secret?

He decided to apply psychology to slavery and in turn, socially redirected anger and hostility through the juxtaposition of basic needs/slave ownership linkage – positioning him (or anyone else implementing his tactics) directly in the driver's seat (control).

His psychological tactics pitted the slaves against one another:

-Light skin vs. Dark skin
-Old vs. young
-Men vs. women

If you read his paper, you'll also notice that he uses both; a selection process as well as limits (language limits, etc) – that prevent the slaves from attaining higher "needs".

In turn, these higher "needs" are supplemented with fear (of beatings, death, family brutality/raping) – and so fear becomes law, mindset and life for these people.

In addition to the fear tactics is the limiting of knowledge and information – which is the same thing our government and other governments are doing right now to retain control (info=power).

We should have the right to know historical information, skewed statistics (especially in the medical field), and above all – we should have the right to know where our tax dollars are going, what everyone's salary is within any and every branch of the government, what their bonuses are based on and how much they are compensated, all the

way to what projects are being funded – down to the last penny.

The government and higher powers think we are fools and play us as such through their media frenzy instead of incubating us with knowledge and arming us with reassurance and security through transparency.

They wouldn't have a problem with transparency
if there wasn't something to hide...

Some people claim that Willie Lynch is a hoax - but as you know, there will always be naysayers to argue a point.

Either way, whether real or hoax, the mentality is real – and it's been fostered through our past, present and bred into our future.

When I say "our history" – I'm not referring to the US. I mean "our history" as a global presence – human beings.

Take a look at the Spanish, Chinese or early Egyptian rulers – many would try to destroy all previous art, text, documentation, tablets, pottery, tapestry, culture, etc – all in a sole effort to contain the truth and then become it.

If you can contain all evidence of truth,
then you can become it.

The same destruction of history happened all over the world at one time or another – for the Mayans and other tribes alike, it was the Spanish reigning down havoc.

This is our history – revisionistic as it may be.

Fast forward from the 1700's and Willie to the mid 1960's and we'll see another exhibition of control through exploitation and deception.

CLOWARD AND PIVEN

Richard A Cloward and Frances F Piven promoted their strategy first in 1966, with intentions to bring down the government by turning it on itself.

Through the exploitation of "chinks in the armor", a systematic breakdown could be implemented and leveraged for control. The events that lead up to the plan's

true execution seem long and drawn out – strategic like chess – but when it's time for the change to occur, it will be like a game dodgeball as we avoid the debris.

Then, as the system crumbles – it is rebuilt seemingly overnight with pre-laid "contingency" plans.

In brief, the Cloward-Piven strategy suggests the following:

~Systematic, Strategic, or Manufactured crisis that is leveraged for takeover of privatized industry or leveraged for radical change (9/11 possibly?)

~Overloading systems so they break (welfare, electoral, etc)

~Increasing Federal control (over state and individual)

~Inundating the Government with impossible financial burdens (bailouts)

If there's any doubt that this strategy doesn't work, please do your research on the Cloward-Piven strategy and you'll see their results echoing from the past and ultimately resounding in our future.

Shortly after the debut of this strategy in 1966, an implementation of it was executed in New York – a push to get people on welfare in order to 'tank the system'.

As a result, the number of people on welfare from 1965 to 1974 went from a little over 4 million to nearly 11 million – forcing New York City to declare bankruptcy in 1975, nearly taking the rest of New York down with it.

+50 YEARS LATER

'Cloward and Piven' is still happening today – take a look at bailouts. Would any government entity come to our rescue (as the American public) if we went belly up?

No.

And you can bet your ass if they did, there would be so much red tape tied to that loan that we would never see any of it for wasteful spending (AIG vacationing on bailout money – WTF).

Our economies (the US as well as other economies around the globe) are beginning to fail. The reason they are failing is because of the people in control, the laws that put them there or enabled them (or have been exploited by them), and ultimately because the lack of transparency enabled their corruption that has been bred into the system.

Speaking about the bailouts – why would you continue to let someone run a company (off a government bailout) when they ran it into the ground in the first place?

Wouldn't a leadership change be in order with a strict spending policy on the bailout money?

Is no one else pissed that our money has been foolishly given away at whim and we only suffer from it while the 1% in control prospers – the middle and lower classes have been fucked so long our asses whistle like beer bottles in the wind.

Hear our symphony.

The bailouts were close to the tune of +$7 trillion dollars. And we're ok with this?

We couldn't spend $7 trillion dollars on the improvement of the American publics' quality of life proactively, but we can reactively write these types of checks for assholes who go on vacation with some of the money?

We already looked at how much 1 billion and 42 billion represent in real-world applications like jobs or tangible goods – 1 trillion dollars is almost 24x the impact that we looked at with 42 billion dollars.

PS - 7 trillion is 168x the financial impact... that's 280 million electric cars for the US (with only 310 million citizens).

Where will our economy, our processes and our infrastructure break? What's going to be the straw that broke the camel's back?

If you push a system to its breaking point and strain it until collapse or implosion, you can swoop in afterwards and redesign and re-engineer the entire thing.

Additionally, if YOU were designing a hierarchal system from the ground up, don't you think you'd put yourself at

the top of it, just as they have positioned themselves?

THEY & THEM

We often hear the ambiguous 'they' or 'them' without certainty in context. 'They' could represent people of any congregation, consortium, fellowship, brotherhood, interest group or governing body.

Sometimes 'they' or 'them' cannot be publicly defined – the people pulling the strings, playing government officials like pawns, shadow governments, the wealthy and powerful (Bilderbergs, Mellons, etc).

Those that believe our President is in control of our country are sadly mistaken, for he is just another pawn playing the game.

Everyone has their place in the game, although we are all grunts in comparison to the ones at the top – the elite – the 1%.

To clarify and ensure you are not misinterpreting me for believing everyone is against us – I am simply saying there

is a higher order controlling the countries of the world besides their superficial leadership or Presidents – and that broken processes have been put in place, legally, to be exploited by those involved in the same processes every day to self or single-sourced-benefit.

If you want to know more about this I urge you to do your research on the Illluminati, Freemasons, Skull and Bones, and other organizations that "don't exist".

Corruption is running rampant in our systems.

We, the people, need to be at a maturity level capable of sustaining moral, ethical and social responsibilities to the point of proliferation of our quality of life and in time, quantity of life.

With the previous being understood, I submit that we can neither socially evolve nor maintain our current state without a redefinition of systems and processes that are focused on the governed body as well as new leadership to uphold the ideals of transparency and the best interests of those governed, followed by those involved, in that order.

Transparency and information.

ECONOMIC HITMEN

In the '70s the US employed the services of Economic Hitmen.

Basically, their job was to go to countries less developed and offer funding and assistance to their infrastructure.

In turn, we would want them to pay the money back with interest, in such a way that it was impossible for them to pay us back.

Once the country got deep enough into a hole of debt with the US, we would ask them for payment.

They would inform us that they could not pay us and in turn we would reassure them that it's ok not to pay with cash… but we would need SOMETHING in return (ass, grass or cash – no one rides for free).

The 'something' that we received could range anywhere from the privatization of their water, electric or sewage – to building military bases in their backyards.

If they didn't play ball with us – we would kill their leader (covertly) and hope the next would comply out of fear or suffer the same penalty until one was smart enough to play or dumb enough to be led to believe he was calling the shots at the suggestion of higher orders.

If we are willing to extort other countries to gain a tactical and financial advantage – where is our limit? Where do we draw the proverbial line in the sand for our morals and ethics?

More importantly, where has this line in the sand been moved due to social conditioning?

DEPOPULATION

With all the previous examples of control, power and greed – we begin to see a pattern.

This pattern will continue until it is identified on a widespread scale and dealt with in a manner that exemplifies transparency and quality of life.

Which brings us to a moral dilemma dealing with supply vs. demand – what happens when we don't have the supplies to meet the food demands of the world?

Do we react when it's 'too late' and start up concentration camps, killing fields and drowning pools in efforts to save others?

Let's take a closer look at this problem of Earth reaching critical mass.

Our world population is almost 7 billion people right now (6.888 billion to be a little more exact).

The USA is about 4% of the population pie (310 million citizens) while China weighs in nearly 20% of the world pop (1.3 billion citizens).

Remember earlier when I said that the trick with numbers is not giving all the information or putting it in fine print? I left out an important piece of information with the above comment about the US vs. China's population.

Realizing that most Americans don't know how many square miles the US or China occupies, it's possible some

would initially think "they're taking up too much space" – but what if the space they occupy is 5x larger than the US? Would it be so bad if we're proportional?

Ironically enough, in this example both countries are of almost identical size – with the US weighing in at about 3.8 million square miles and China weighing in around 3.7 million.

This means China not only has 5x more citizens as the US, but does so in roughly the same geographical area - talk about cramped.

With the variance of those population numbers (US vs China) yet occupying similar geographical space, you can see how our governments would be interested in depopulation or pop-control.
Before we continue down this path, let's take a second and acknowledge the need for survival and the desire to generate a quality of life greater than ours for our children.

In wanting these things, we must allow that population control is necessary (to some degree) until space travel is feasible and galactic colonization is proliferating.

With that being said, other people must have had the same notions right?

Right.

That's where the Georgia Guidestones come into play.

In 1980, huge stones (over 15 feet high, some weighing over 40,000 pounds each) were erected in Georgia (Elbert County). These huge stones contained 10 'instructions' of some sort, etched into them in numerous languages:

1. *Maintain humanity under 500,000,000*
   in perpetual balance with nature.

2. *Guide reproduction wisely*
   - improving fitness and diversity.

3. *Unite humanity with a living new language.*

4. *Rule passion - faith - tradition*
   - and all things with tempered reason.

5. *Protect people and nations with fair laws and just courts.*

6. *Let all nations rule internally resolving external*
   disputes in a world court.

7. Avoid petty laws and useless officials.

8. Balance personal rights with social duties.

*9. Prize truth - beauty - love - seeking
        harmony with the infinite.*

*10. Be not a cancer on the earth
        - Leave room for nature
            - Leave room for nature.*

These 10 'commandments' if you will were written in Russian, Arabic, Chinese, Hindi, Hebrew, English, Swahili and Spanish. 8 languages – one on each side of the stones, each stone pointing in a different direction (North, South, East and West).

Whoa whoa whoa – back up – that first one up there said to maintain humanity under 500 million? So that's like the US (310) Mexico (110) and Germany (80).

Wow.

And we're almost 7 BILLION people deep now?

Not to mention that the Georgia Guidestones don't look "cheap" – so that means someone with a little money would have had to make the investment – which means they had people backing them... people with money.

Most of these instructions from the Guidestones look agreeable.

Leave room for nature – this should resonate with all of us – a necessary shift in thinking – an awareness of nature and our carbon footprint on a global level.

Depopulation sounds like a bad idea because it sounds a little too pro-active – to the degree that in hearing "depopulation" we could think of Hitler's decision to commit genocide – or possibly the US giving tainted food to third world nations – starving some and drenching others with disease from the tainted food.
Neither of these ideas is acceptable through social responsibility.

The only correct way to manage the population would be to look at all viable options which allow everyone the ability for reproduction but not a free-for-all welfare fling

(8 kids, are you fucking kidding me?) – a humane solution through widespread information.

Anything decided should be communicated to all and not hidden for one to discover years later.

For example if governments put chemicals in our foods or water sources that made us less fertile (fluoride) – I'd rather know about that up front than later, wouldn't you?

Lucky for us that the fields of Science and Technology are advancing at a pace that will enable solutions so that depopulation will be a thing of the past – merely a socially primitive idea.

– Chapter 3 –

AMERICAN PSYCHO(LOGY)

This chapter is inspired by the American mindset that I see people living out everyday – the life of entitlement, court-whores, profit-focused leadership and politics in business… and these are but a few examples of the everyday mindsets many US citizens fall victim to.

I believe that this mindset is merely a response from conditioning and intentional misguidance, and it can be corrected.

After reading the next few sections, it's hard not to feel like we've somehow 'missed the mark' and gone astray as a society, where these examples not only occur, but are commonplace.

We're going to take a look at how the system is manipulated – by either faulty design or faulty leadership.

TREATMENTS AND CURES

We took a look at some numbers earlier in this book, with the US Prescription Biz worth about $290 billion bucks – that's a lot of junkies.

You need a symptom to have a treatment or a cure – and there's money in both – however sustainable revenue can only be generated from repeat customers.

Meaning? No cure.

Only treatments and ways to prolong a disease or symptom, possibly causing side effects (residual /cumulative/collateral damage) tethering you tighter to medical needs (prescriptions, treatments, therapy, operations).

You have just become a cash cow.

Why are we allowing someone's quality of life to suffer by prolonging their ailment? Shouldn't each of us be entitled to quality healthcare? Shouldn't we be entitled to minimal physical suffering and expedited wellness?

They want us to get sick, to be susceptible, to keep coming back to line their pockets – if you do your research about the fast food industry and weight loss food additives (Aspartame / Olestra) you will be surprised about what's you're ingesting and how it's affecting you.

At some point, one must stand up and say
that the course of the ship is lost,
that the current command is insufficient and incapable,
that new leadership must be sought.

This new establishment must include foundations which resonate
within each of us;
inalienable rights and symmetry with nature... and with "right" being
defined and qualified by 'right for self, right for others,
and right for nature' mentality.

Is this not the most patriotic of duties: to acknowledge when the moral compass of leadership no longer leads in the direction of well-being but instead towards the cliffs of deception and the bitter-cold waters of debt below?

When isolated power is granted in coves of popularity contests, quid pro quo mentality and incentivized with kick-backs, donations, gifts and so much more it would make you sick - something needs to be addressed.

When are we going to begin to question where our money has been going, what has been happening behind the scenes – when will we demand transparency, consideration and justice?

"We hold these truths to be self-evident, that all men are created equal, that they are endowed by their Creator with certain unalienable Rights, that among these are Life, Liberty and the pursuit of Happiness.

— That to secure these rights, Governments are instituted among Men, deriving their just powers from the consent of the governed,

— That whenever any Form of Government becomes destructive of these ends, it is the Right of the People to alter or to abolish it, and to institute new Government, laying its foundation on such principles and organizing its powers in such form, as to them shall seem most likely to effect their Safety and Happiness. Prudence, indeed, will dictate that Governments long established should not be changed for light and transient causes"
- Declaration of Independence

Safety and Happiness – are we really a safe nation when the media utilizes fear tactics to control John Q Public?

A happy nation? With close to 30 million people (about 10% of the US population) on antidepressants, I don't think we're a very happy nation. But then again, what's a good baseline for happiness?

What's an acceptable number? 1 in 100? 1 in 1,000?

That's where I think we should be closer to – at a minimum – 1 in 1,000 people depressed and still I'd say that's not really 'acceptable'.

Possibly 1 in 10,000 – although it would be optimal that 1 in a million or higher although these numbers are probably not practical at our current evolutionary state – for now, we should strive for 1 in 1,000 people depressed instead of 1 in 10.

Why is everyone so unhappy? Can it be the bombardment of the media? The negative influences around us like drugs, guns, rock 'n roll? Satanists even?

I believe one cause is over-focusing on people's basic needs; food, housing, sex (sex sells, right?), security (with

military strength) – and neglecting to take responsibility for guidance and development (in an open-minded manner) – which comes back to social responsibility.

We need to revise what isn't working and change whatever is creating social unrest or discontent – we need to alleviate the root causes.

Imagine what we could achieve with transparency,
because without it, we're all in the dark
and transparent to leadership.

MONEY – FAKE ON EVERY LEVEL

From conception to execution, the currency we use every day is just a façade – the idea of money (just as the idea of time) is a mere concept that we have created and adopted to continue our socio-economic (r)evolution.

The general public consensus is that we (the good ol' USA) print up our wonderfully bland green money and send it out the door to a bank – this would be a fairly close assumption of the process, but a couple key points have been left out.

How about the fact that The Federal Reserve is privately owned? Our government purchases our currency from independent bankers (wtf?) and we in turn give bonds of equal value to these bankers – and the icing on the cake is that the money is loaned to the US Government with interest on it. YGBSM (You gotta be shitting me).

Why aren't we printing our OWN money and circulating it instead of taking loaned money with interest? I believe Andrew Jackson warned us of this…

If you ever want to know how our financial system operates you should start at the beginning: Modern Money Mechanics, a document built with a self-destruct. Specifically interesting is the part about our system being a Fractional Reserve system.

What this means (roughly) is that at any given time only 10% of the actual amount of loaned money must be physically stored at that particular bank and the other 90% can be re-loaned out as an entirely new loan.

This can go on again and again with new loan thresholds lessening 10% each time…

As a bank, if you had 10 million dollars, you'd have to keep 10% as reserves, but could loan the other 90% (9 million) back out as a new loan.

By using this process, we create inherent inflation as we have the potential with 10 million dollars to create about 90 million in new loans.

That's technically 100 million dollars worth of debt (as the US has borrowed some of these dollars from the Federal Reserve – a private group of bankers) – plus interest.

So basically, our system was setup as an 'impossible' system – the foundation is not solid or secure and will be difficult to sustain for future generations, especially as we evolve into a digitized future and press on as a unified species. We need to start thinking about the future, now.

RIDER, DIE

Riders: customary legislation that is passed in connection with congressionally passed bills.

Here's the catch – the riders to bills usually have little to

do with it (hmmm like a gun law inside of a school bill or inheritance tax law inside of a health care bill?) – usually 'controversial' legislation is tacked on as a rider.

Is there not a more pure form of corruption – the IF/WHEN social programming? A quid-pro-quo favor-trading governing body.

YGBSM – I thought "if you scratch my back, I'll scratch yours" was just a mind state for sexually active teenagers – yet it's alive and well within our leadership.

Legislation should be passed individually, to maintain transparency and allow peer review with complete understanding, for the betterment of the governed body.

The elected representatives need to be concerned with our general and future well-being, safety, security, with focus on the elimination of social barriers and walls – as well as focusing on the quality of life (happiness) of the governed body.

GIMME GIMME GIMME

Besides the tit-for-tat mentality within our legislative branch and the profit-focused Corporate America, we have become conditioned, as a society, on many levels (sex, language, customs, etc).

In the next few sections, we're going to look at the ripple effects of the conditioning we have been subjected to – and conditioning for holidays, gifts and seasonal customs are no exception... so while we're taking a look at some of the psychological aspects of Americans, let's take a brief look at Christmas conditioning.

What's the question everyone asks you after Christmas?

"What did you get for Christmas?"

Questions that leap to my mind when I think about this phrase: Why are we so infatuated with acquisition? Why do we always want to know what other people received for Christmas (as if their acquisition would benefit us)? ...or do we ask this question because we have been conditioned to associate happiness with the receipt of

gifts?

It's incredible that our society is so focused on measuring success by materialistic gain that we have forgotten to ask questions like "what did you give for Christmas"…

Conditioning occurs throughout our lives with influence from marketing and media sources, as well as social constructs. The 'positive gain' to conditioning is 'consistency in governed-body behavior'… but what happens when the governed body gets too big or goes off course?

Furthermore, as we breed traits like dominance, greed, neglect, anger, materialism and entitlement, we see the effects within society and the victims of the system.

Victims are not always victims – as we have also been conditioned to be victimized, placing blame in all directions and taking zero responsibility. Eventually, victims of the system end up as leaders of tomorrow… which is the cycle we need to stop.

COFFEE

(CAUTION - HOT)

You might remember a court case back around 1992/94 involving some yellow arched company and some hot coffee. If you haven't heard about this yet let me bring you up to speed...

An elderly lady (late 70's) went through the drive-thru at said company and purchased coffee. She was trying to add sugar/cream to her coffee when it spilled on her – giving her third degree burns on her buttocks, genitals and thighs – which later required skin grafts.

This coffee was obviously heated to a temperature that was unsafe, which is why she sued for over 2 million dollars – in the end actually being awarded a little over $600,000.

Let's get the facts straight on a few things before we jump to conclusions – the vehicle was STOPPED.

That's right – her grandson had driven her and had pulled

the vehicle over after they left the drive-thru so that she could safely take the top off her coffee and add her sugar and cream – but she steadied the hot coffee between her legs.

I understand that the woman was burned and I have sympathy for her (for the burns as well as her lack of intelligence and dexterity) – but common sense tells us *not to open a hot coffee between our legs* – COME ON PEOPLE.

The temperature of the coffee was in debate, stating that the temperature was way too high around 185 degrees. For the non-java readers – coffee brewing is an art (numerous ways to brew coffee, numerous ways to enjoy it).

When you brew coffee, the optimal temperature is 195 to 205 degrees.

The reason the temperature needs to be so high is for the oils to come out of the ground up bean – which is the whole reason you're making/enjoying coffee in the first place – the oils from the bean that produce the flavors/aromas/effects from coffee that you enjoy.

So we've determined that "good" coffee is brewed at 195 to 205 degrees – and when you transfer this fresh coffee into a Styrofoam container (which is fantastic at insulating as this lady found out) – what do you think would happen?

The coffee will stay HOT.

You purchased coffee. Not iced coffee – but COFFEE.

The best part of the story is that the lady originally only wanted $20,000 to settle but the heartless corporate monster offered her a measly $800.00 – eight hundred dollars.

What's the root cause here? Her lack of care in prying the top off? Her lack of planning (use a firm surface – not a seat that's squishy)? Is it McDonald's fault for keeping the coffee too hot?

I believe she has been conditioned (and victimized) by the system to believe she is entitled to suing, she is entitled to financial compensation for her pain and agony, which she has been conditioned to believe is NOT her fault - as it

always has to be an external fault.

…

Is it the people, courts and the systems in place making these decisions or is it the media and the people who control the media who have initiated this conditioning?

As I've said before, I am sorry this unfortunate event caused her pain and a lessened quality of life, but you have to use a little common sense throughout life – and we should be TEACHING common sense as well (difficult as it may be to teach, there are activities that can reinforce the correct behavior).

But why don't we REALLY step back, burn the box and paint a whole new picture?

How about this same scenario goes down with a different rule book? The same events play out with the lady using her legs to steady the cup while they were parked so she could pry the top off – and she still gets 3rd degree burns.

But instead of her trying to "blame" (as we have become a nation of victims – blaming everything and accepting zero responsibility) – how about her medical costs are taken

care of – as well as a little extra paid for her time/inconvenience – all paid for BY THE GOVERNMENT (taking care of the citizens).

This could be a reality – one where we don't have to fear repercussions from truth – one that ensures quality of life for all – one where the "average" life expectancy equalizes globally, allowing quantity of life increases in addition to quality surges.

CORPORATE FAIRY TALE

Next, we're going to go off on a tangent and take a look at Corporate America's mindset…

Suppose you work at XYZ corporation selling appliances.

You're a district manager responsible for over $6 million dollars in revenue.

You have 5 inside sales people, an administrator and a driver. Your district is profitable, bringing at least one and a half million dollars to the bottom line (pure profit). Here's where the fun part of the "corporate world" comes into

play…

The corporation you work for has a basic rule that every associate in a "revenue generating" position should generate 1.25 million/year (average).

So you've got 5 inside sales divided by 6 million which comes out to about 1.25 million for each associate. No – tht too shabby - right on the money... thankfully your admin is a support role and doesn't fall under the classification of a revenue generator.

Oh, did I forget to mention that your delivery driver makes you about $100,000 each year – which means he's a revenue generator and we need to divide that 6 million by SIX people... bringing the revenue per associate to 1 million…

"Not good enough" corporate booms down through the chain of command. "Heavy" is the term circulated… and you need to let 1 person go.

Obviously you can't give up your inside sales, so you make the best decision in a bad situation – you let your driver go (which only generates 100k).

This doesn't seem very 'fair' when you consider the facts – the story behind the story. These are the things which need to be considered in all circumstances – ones that can be verified and are positive or synergistic.

Here's the details that make this matter:

- *Your driver was LOVED by every customer (in a repeat customer business) exhibiting strong customer service skills*

- *Your driver would do more than expected – as customers requested him to offload the heavy equipment and move it into their warehouse, which he loaded and offloaded by hand and dolly.*

- *Instead of being "tail-gate only" service, which was all he was required to do... he went the extra mile and supported your company. (Remember – your company is only as good as the marketing, reputation and people that interface with the end users. Your front line is quintessential to your success.)*

- *Your driver cost you $25k – but generated you about $100k – easily paying for himself with the revenue he generated.*

- *Your driver knew the routes and was efficient*

This is a typical corporate example (politics, numbers, accountability not held in the correct places - or perhaps just bad timing and poor planning for long term longevitiy or new trending)... but these events exist on every level – legal, insurance, health, media, politics, religious and government…

An often misused business practice is incentives – motivational dollars set aside for agreed-upon metrics being achieved. This includes staying under operational costs, maintaining margins and other assorted metrics that drive corporations to become cut-throat on lower levels.

Keeping the company profitable for the shareholders is important – oftentimes more important than the people in the company that make a difference (on the front lines) instead of cutting money in areas that deserve to be cut (overhead that adds no value).

It's difficult to lose good employees over politics like the above referenced story and then watch the same company piss away thousands of dollars on alcohol and entertainment.

Instead of tightening down on spending in other areas, a

good employee (the "face" of your company) was chewed up and spit out by politics, process and generalization.

Downsizing is necessary in certain circumstances, but not for political reasons.

Church and State shouldn't mix and neither should Business and Politics (Politrix)...

YOUR 500K (TIME'S TICKIN)

In this chapter we have discussed a few of the psychological aspects that play important roles in day to day American life, including entitlement to sue, quid-pro-quo mentality for laws and greed in corporations – but none of these would be possible without the social construct of Time – the most precious commodity.

It's something that doesn't even exist, yet we constantly need more of it. We have made Time a commodity.

We're going to take a closer look at how much time we've got in order to see why this mindset is so critical to some...

Average life expectancy in the US is about 78 (this number is from about 2008-2009 – back in the '60s the average life expectancy in the US was about 70 – good thing it's going up and it's nice to see that it's steady).

Before we look at how much time you've got left, let's take a look at how the US compares to some of the other countries for average life expectancy:

Afghanistan	44	Peru	73
Germany	80	Switzerland	82
Pakistan	66	North Korea	67
China	73	South Korea	81
Uganda	52	Mexico	75
Japan	83	Ethiopia	55
India	63	Spain	81

Not too shabby for the good ol' US of A, eh?

But if you think about those 78 years, the first 5 are a blur, the next 10 are physically and socially developmental, and the next 3-5 you're coming into your own (and probably "the best years of your life" simply put by a man wiser than I).

So really the first 20 years (rough average) are used to achieve some sort of homeostasis and proficiency of skills and understandings… which leaves you with about 58 years to enjoy.

58 years sounds like a lot, doesn't it?

It's a little over 21,000 days or a little over 500,000 hours (next time you're watching a shitty movie I bet you'll reconsider the 2 hour investment into it knowing that your 500k's counting down).

Keep in mind – that's not 500,000 hours you have to enjoy… that's 500,000 hours to be alive – your body still needs things like sleep (1/3 of your life if you sleep 8 hours a day).

Let's assume you get 7 hours of sleep on average (which includes you sleeping 10 or 11 hours on the weekends or on your days off and only getting 3 or 4 hours here and there with an average of about 7 hours per night)…

So 7 hours a day completely gone and you barely got to enjoy it (unless it was a really good dream).

7 hours a day turns into 2,555 hours a year slept away, which turns into 148,000 in those 58 years (roughly 1/3) but don't forget, you're not independently wealthy, you've got to work too!

That's about 40 hours a week or 2080 estimated in an 'hourly work-year' – coming out to 120,000 (lifetime) hours worked (+/- overtime and retirement).

500,000 hours total
-148,000 hours slept away
<u>-120,000</u> hours worked away

232,000 hours left

232,000 hours left, right? Wrong.

How about showering? On average Americans spend 5-10 minutes in the shower each day – not to mention using the 'facilities'. All in all you could assume 35 minutes of your day will be spent in the bathroom (either in the shower, brushing your teeth, flossing, shaving, etc) – and don't forget about eating…

On average, people spend about 60 minutes a day preparing and eating their food. So that's 95 minutes a day when you combine the bathroom and food time investments – 31,000 more hours down the drain (literally).

200,000 hours.

That's what you're basically down to. A little over 22 years for you to do whatever you'd like.

Oh, but don't forget that this doesn't include idle time – waiting in lines, waiting in rush-hour traffic or driving to and from work (every day), grocery shopping, college... and how about when you add in kids or a loved one into the mix?

After this exercise, it's apparent that time is fleeting and we must capitalize on it when plentiful.

We must shift our thinking to encompass social responsibility and quality of life in all decision making

(individual or made by governing bodies).

Life's too short not to enjoy it – let's enable this.

Chapter 4

T T M F D
(TEAR THIS MF'er DOWN)

EXAMPLE 1

"You have the right to remain silent. Anything you say can and will be used against you in a court of law."

This is the beginning of the "Miranda Rights" – read by every law enforcement officer in the US – but does anyone else see something wrong with this picture besides me?

Anything you say… can… and will be used against you.

The verbiage is worded in such a way that 'the system' wants to incarcerate and victimize its citizens and will do so by any means necessary. Which means if you're telling the truth, then it can and will be used against you?

How fucked up is that. Thankfully not all police/law enforcement are corrupt and bad (many of them are good-hearted people which have a high caliber of social respect and social responsibility – but are hindered by process or blinded with misinformation).

EXAMPLE 2 – The Health Bill

Now this is a true YGBSM moment. Let me get this straight – we're letting people make decisions for us, the governed body (310 million people), that affects us short term and long term – and these people don't even read the fucking thing?

It's +1000 pages – and they vote on it without reading it first? Those people need to be expeditiously pulled out of office and replaced – every last worthless one of them that signed off.

This is an outrage for our country to be run as such – signing off on legislation without first understanding what is being signed.

Here are a few gems the people who came up with the Health Bill included:

> • *Near the end of your life, your Advanced Care Planning Consultant will determine your condition and as it deteriorates, treatment will be rationed and you could be ordered for an 'end of life' plan.*

In short – 'they' decide how your life plays out in the final stages – sweet deal huh? What's next – death squads going door to door?

- *All non-US citizens will be provided with free healthcare services – instead of taxing these citizens a little more and giving them an incentive to become an American (isn't that how to incentivize someone?).*

Incentive = the more someone repeats the correct behavior, the more they get rewarded. You don't see Sam's Club, BJ's Wholesale or any other club membership giving out lower prices and perks to non-members over the regular members, do you? WTF is going on here?

- *Government Healthcare employees will have access to all of your financial and personal records – talk about invasion of privacy*

- *Government-set wages*

There's much more in the health bill (and a beautiful 'trickle down' effect from it), as it's over 1000 pages of legalese.

I can see the need for a health reform, it's not that I don't – I'm just wondering what aspects of the healthcare system will be affected from the poor process planning or one-sided reasoning?

If the government sets the wages and adopts the "no child left behind" policy for the doctors of the future, then the

quality of healthcare we may be getting might be a little 'hit or miss'. I'm banking on more misses than hits.

If we crossed the Health Bill with the Cloward and Piven strategy and then stepped back to view the synergy, I wonder what that'd look like….

Health Bill numbers:

- *Close to $1 trillion in costs (over about 10 years)*

- *Insurance coverage to +30 million Americans*

(remember – 310 million in all of the US – that's nearly 10% that were living without insurance that will now have it – sounds like when New York City went bankrupt with all the people they recruited to sign up for welfare)

And don't forget the 7 trillion in bailout…

Hmmm maybe there's something going on here? I believe you'll find Obama, ACORN and Cloward and Piven linked numerous times if you do a little research, but don't take my word for it… please do a quick search and read up.

With all the secrecy, information hoarding and corruption from within, it's difficult to imagine that power will ever reverse flow from the 1% back to the other 99%...

In turn, there aren't many ways to "take the power back" as Rage Against The Machine put it.

- *You can steal it back (but that requires a massive infrastructure, planning, resources, capital, etc)*

- *You can overthrow what's already in place (also requiring a massive infrastructure, planning, resources, capital, weaponry, manpower, etc)*

- *You can 'Cloward and Piven' it and then opportunistically take advantage of a manufactured crisis (also requiring a shit-ton of resources. Note — "shit-ton" is a highly technical, industry term in this case)*

The only other ways that power will change hands would be divine, alien intervention or a natural disaster of cataclysmic proportions - like a solar flare which emits a huge EMP (electro-magnetic pulse) that knocks out all of our electronics, glacial ice melting causing massive flooding, a super-volcano under Yellowstone National Park erupting, a comet smashing into our planet, etc.

SOCIAL RESPECT / SOCIAL RESPONSIBILITY

If you acknowledge the fundamental right of another human being to be alive and their right to happiness and additional unalienable freedoms, or their right to individual beliefs and culture – then you have social respect.

We need to embrace this type of respect instead of harboring anger and hate for anything we deem 'different'.

We have forgotten social responsibilities in this country (and other countries too, I'm sure) – corruption knows no boundaries through greed and power – and you cannot tell me that this very trait does not echo through the halls of our justice and legislative branches and governing bodies.

There is corruption around us at all times – but we are not looking at why the corruption is in place.

The first reason is that we're tolerating it, as a society – as a species. It seems like isolated tolerance but the truth is often blurred and spun by the media in such a way so that it doesn't change the public's view of; government, religious leaders, corporations, etc…

Consideration appears to be a thing of the past or a treat found only in isolated moments throughout your life – why have we become so wrapped up within ourselves?

We walk around with blinders on… to the point when you drive through parking lots, people don't even look left or right before crossing (granted pedestrians have the right of way, but wouldn't you take the social responsibility to look both ways to ensure your own life's safety – taking RESPONSIBILITY for your actions, regardless of fault)…

This is because they have been conditioned to do so - they know that consequences will befall the driver that hits them as a pedestrian and that they can "sue", therefore they don't have to look left or right - they are "entitled".

When you merge on the interstate people either don't move over to let you in or drive so incredibly slow that it makes it difficult to merge (getting on the interstate doing 40mph will get you and other people into accidents – merge WITH traffic).

When drivers don't move over for you to merge, they aren't always getting off at the exit – sometimes they just don't care to let you in…

They don't want to give up their "spot", as they are entitled to it.

Luckily, not everyone is an asshole – there's still some good people left out there – probably the same individuals reading this book and looking for a change.

People can only take so much bullshit in their lives before even a good person will break somewhere, sometime.

I believe we have taken enough and are at a position where we must decide what is best for the people and not the 1% of the wealthy and rich controlling our lives.

GETTING TO THE ROOT CAUSE

So if it's not the drugs, the music, the video games, prostitution – why do we place the blame there? Why do we continually justify our actions through 'limited logic' or one sided mentality and narrow-minded tunnel vision?

Our evolution has gone through many transformations, but we have forgotten (or have been led to forget) some critical needs:

- *the need for knowledge*
- *the need for transparency*

Further spiraling out of control, we allow a government to tax us to death and to manufacture a system around us which clearly separates the wealthy from the poor.

We have only two classes of people in our society – the wealthy and everyone else. Why are we not re-evaluating our infrastructure to see where we can cut costs to give back to the public or provide relief or overall quality of life increases?

Why are we not identifying broken processes or efforts spent in the wrong direction and fixing them or removing them?

It seems as if we are continually focusing on the symptom instead of the cause…

We have substituted POLITICAL correctness for SOCIAL correctness.

I've heard remarks from people in passing, regarding the current state of affairs and acknowledging that the system is corrupt – but since they are cannot do anything about it, they decide not to worry about it. I think we all feel like we're in the same boat when you step back and say "but what can I do about it?"

Some would tell you that a rally or speech would help –

others claim that voting is the only way for change.
I submit to you that voting does not, cannot and will not
work for our infrastructure today. Voting is simply a
popularity contest for a figurehead who holds no real
power.

If voting was to truly work, we should vote individually
for a single piece of legislation and have each citizen
actually vote – a near impossible feat today. I'm unsure of
what will enable us to spark change – unfortunately I
believe it will need to be a near-catastrophic event
(possibly even global) before power shifts hands from the
corrupt to the everyman.

It's important to note that the "powershift" is metaphorical
because we're really just defining the FOCUS of the
governing bodies shifting from greed to social
responsibility and social respect with unification on first a
national and then a global scale.

As a creative solution to enable everyone to vote, how
about the government issues a "voting computer" to
everyone in the US?

Sound impossible? Let's take a look…

We've already covered the fact that there's 310 million
people in the US and that 75 million of those 310 million

are 17 and under.

This leaves us with 235 million Americans able to vote (keep in mind, not everyone would NEED a laptop, but this might not be a functioning laptop in all regards and would potentially be a secure laptop specifically for voting purposes or 'social' purposes – not *socializing* purposes).

If you remember a few years ago (around 2006-2008) there was a non-profit initiative called OLPC – One Laptop Per Child.

The goal of this initiative was to create a rugged laptop that was wireless, used minimal energy, was cost effective and could connect students, teachers and families in the most remote locations.

The target cost of this machine was somewhere around $100 (starting a little under $200, with hopes to reduce costs down to $50 per laptop in the future). If you can create a bare-bone laptop for $100, we'd be looking at a 23.5 billion dollar investment to give a laptop to every US adult, making voting more accessible (and more convenient) than ever.

Not to mention that we could put a laptop in EVERY American's hands for 31 billion… and we're pissing away 42 billion dollars each year on a fucking war on pot.

TTMFD - FOR DUMMIES

We need to bring all the suppressed secrets to light in a controlled, methodical way. This is the social responsibility of the governing bodies (religious, scientific, economic, political, etc) and equally important if not MORE so is the social responsibility of the governed body (us) to not react emotionally and physically to anyone involved with these suppressed secrets (government workers, police officers, hospitals, doctors, etc).

This is a two-way street : we get answers, direction, unification – but maintain composure, emotional control and physical restraint.

The guilty parties in the government or power positions must step down once the secrets are out – my apologies, but if you've abused your power – you must step down, as you are in no position to lead. If you will not step down, we will bring you down – such is our duty expressed in the Declaration of Independence.

The Declaration also reads "Governments long established should not be changed for light and transient causes" – I propose to you that public health and safety (fluoridation of our water, known chemicals that cause cancer/breast cancer that is approved in our foods, etc) is such a cause...

as is the 1 in 10 citizens depressed – does this sound like a government concerned with public health, safety and happiness?

Additionally I would lobby that our psyche needs an immediate rebalance – 40 million US adult citizens with some type of anxiety disorder (about **18%** of the adult population –

nearly 1 in 5)

This appears to be an urgent social matter to contend with as life is stimuli and response, cause and effect – so something must be triggering 18% of the adult US population to feel this way – there must be a solution as well…

Obviously the way things are going is the wrong direction.

We have severely gone off course with free enterprise as the puppeteers buy the future through lobbyists, powerplays, greed and legislation.

Going back to the fact that the Declaration of Independence set the pretenses of government decisions to be based on safety and happiness of citizens - let's not forget about eating disorders (bulimia, anorexia, binge) which make up about 4.5% of the US pop – and another 4% or so that are spastic little ADHD energizer bunnies.

When you add up all these numbers, you start to get an idea that we're really fucked up as a country. This is a very serious problem in my opinion – 4 + 4.5 + 18 = 26.5%

1 in 4 of us are depressed, *scared of people or places,*

*or riding the **Fingertrain to Prettyville**.*

Absolutely unacceptable… and the solution in the good ol' US? To medicate them.

Hmmm sounds like a great idea – look at all those jobs and the pure revenue! Pharmaceutical costs are usually dirt cheap for the actual 'medicine' – it's the years of R&D that cost the most – so once a drug is on the market and has paid back the R&D costs, it's almost pure profit which means a quick payback and a potential to score big - especially if you patent a medication that the government requires (vaccinations, flu shots, etc).

The medical field really bangs out a win win with the

pharmaceutical end of things in conjunction with the shrinks that get to tell you what you already know – and then give you a pill to make it go away – cyclical.

Pass legislation to gain more and more control, use media to intimidate the public and use fear for control – drive citizens to depressive states – then medicate them… rinse repeat.
It's as simple as that – and at the same time unfathomably complex.

So how do we break this cycle? Information.

WIKILEAKS

By now, you've probably heard something on the news or at the watercooler about WikiLeaks and how they are 'leaking' sensitive information to the public – or perhaps how they should be shut-down due to their sharing of military information… but one thing's for certain – they're on a mission to educate anyone with an internet connection and who is willing to read.

These people at WikiLeaks deserve some praise in my opinion, as they are truly patriots of this country – bringing transparency and justice which follows.

WikiLeaks has been around since 2007 but recently released the motherload of confidential documents – to the tune of about 250,000…
Quite impressive.

It is the social responsibility of the public, the governed body, to support organizations like WikiLeaks for their efforts to bring justice back to our country – and the only way to bring justice is to educate the masses so they are aware of what's going on.

Information is power… and the only thing that can allow a governed body to wake up from their medicated naps.

I understand that these documents are classified and I believe that everyone has the right to privacy – although I don't believe there is a necessity for such privacy in business, nor religion, science, health or government.

The public has the right to know since the public is the end user / consumer / driving economic force (without us, they couldn't exist).

The lines for transparency shall be drawn distinctly between public and private matters by definition of "currency exchange" or "leadership / governed body relationship".

One point to clarify – I do not condone releasing military information that pinpoints the locations of our troops. All other sensitive information, cover-ups, technology, reports, etc should be provided to the public.

SUMMATION

Taking all previous information discussed into account, it's undeniable that we are in for change one way or another.

Our system cannot remain in this pseudo-homeostasis for much longer without something breaking, imploding or giving way…

It's possible that a massive event will spark the chain of events that gives the people currently in power an opportunistic advantage to merge the US with Canada and Mexico, ultimately looking to unite the world (under power mongers that do not celebrate social responsibility or social respect).
Perhaps we continue with our current state of corruption, injustice, secrecy and oppression – until every system fails and global anarchy ensues…

Contrary to the previous reactive and self-victimized possibilities, we, the people, will slowly unify as we share information and investigate the unknown, uncovering truths that shall set us free as we define what future leadership should look like and tearing the currently broken leadership down.
Transparency, in technical execution, is simple – although the dynamics of it are complex. What I mean by this is that the information to make these governing bodies "transparent" only needs to be uploaded to a website with a simple and intuitive interface – as well as public domain access (free for all). Open the files.

News and physical publications will carry the information further through targeted demographics and social circles.

But that doesn't address how we deal with the information released or how we (the people) interact with our infrastructure.

As I've said before, it is our social responsibility as the people being governed to not react in a physical manner (riots, chaos, anarchy) – this would be a sure method of self-destruction.

We would rebuild after a self-destruct like that, but the pain that our children would endure in the process would

echo in future generations. Emotional reactions have been tolerated for too long – now is the time for self control as well as change.

If we were to redesign the system – we would need to define the new goals and infrastructure before the old one was taken down – a transition of systems.
Again, the goal of this book is only to spread knowledge, information and ideas – not to completely redesign the system or provide answers. I'm only trying to explore my frustration and share some concepts or thoughts so you can walk away empowered by the information to further your research and educate others.

In the following pages we will look into the future – into what the world will be like with these 'perfect' systems in place.

Chapter 5

TH3 FUTUR3

I M A G I N E for a moment...

Luminous trees will line our roads in the future – providing light to nighttime travelers, thanks to genetic modification.

Oil and gasoline fizzle away into archived history while fully-electric vehicles have their time in the spotlight – though not nearly as long as gasoline powered vehicles did, for travel will be revolutionized rapidly to fusion, quantum and then antimatter.

Travel will become automated on land, sea and air – both for public safety and for maximum efficiency. This automation will include a grid of all vehicles on roads or airspace with location (time/space coordinates) information updated in real-time along with sensors outfitted on every vehicle – monitored to prevent unforeseen accidents in all capacities.

Precaution, prevention and proactive thinking are all innate qualities in the future – direct results from embracing social responsibility. With transparency of corporation, governments, systems and leadership, social

barriers will be removed in society as well.

We will be unified in the future – this is inevitable.

We will remove the ruling factors of greed, war and famine. We will continue to have differences (culture and individuality) – but we will have the social respect for each other in this near future to enable diversity to live side by side without negativity, fear or aggression.

Augmented reality becomes our standardized way of life as computers become intimately integrated into our lives in a new, socially evolutionary way.

Information becomes liquid as it streams to you at will without lag, stutter or storage concerns. This enables us to know specific information about any building, place, date, thing, person, food etc. – including GPS information and navigation… not to mention the possibilities of altering the visuals of the world to enable a new eye on life when desired.

A more customizable life for each of us if desired – changing the colors of what's considered normal (changing the sky to bright green and making the grass yellow for example).

We will have superior biological knowledge about ourselves (and aliens as well) which will increase our quality of life to the max. We will have the ability to ensure

that quadriplegics will be able to walk again, the blind will be able to see and the deaf able to hear.

We will be able to ensure safety and peace of mind to all around as we eliminate physical conflict for governing purposes.

Average life expectancy globally grows to 93, almost simultaneously with lifetime extension drugs and stem cell research paving the way for organ replacement – nearly doubling life expectancy for humans.

Power grids will cease and free energy transmission will begin. Wireless power fuels our world – resonating through the air and ground alike. Batteries are a thing of the past as are 'power outages'.

Communication will be instantaneous and virtually unlimited. We will be connected on shared levels of unimaginable proportions.

Food will evolve into mainstream GM (Genetically Modified) produce, crops and other altered products. This will ensure the products we consume do not cause cancers or other diseases/spoil easily – and in turn strengthening our immune system and providing everything we need to stay optimally nourished.

Food Synthesis will come shortly after the proliferation of GM crops/produce. This will allow the sharing of millions

of cultures without the travel to obtain it (onworld and off).

Cancer will recede and vanish as the truth comes out through massive info-sharing. This will apply to many diseases.

Complex Material Synthesis will become a wave of the future – generating something from almost nothing, with pinpoint detail and absolute control of creation.

Artificial intelligence (A.I.) will increase to the point of self awareness and evolve into a new species with a unique culture – teaching our species further evolutionary steps.

Bio-Mechanical will first become controversy and then a lifestyle choice.

This can often enhance certain physical attributes ranging from eyesight (20/20, infrared and other multi-spectrum analysis modes, digital zoom, image capture) to speed enhancing additions (leg/arm replacements, torque upgrades) and infrastructure/support advancements (bone replacement or altering with nanotube tech for virtually unbreakable bones) in addition to organ replacements or life-support backup systems.

Colonization will be occurring as an every-day thing at one point – as will interactions with species from other star systems. We will learn and harness the powers of black

holes, white holes, antigravity, gravitational time-distortion, time travel, terraforming, antimatter, quantum computing, quantum mechanics and quantum energy.

We will have the ability to travel great distances, measured in light years, without sacrifice to time or health.

As we develop intellectually, our bodies will slowly withdraw muscularly and we will see cranial evolution, due to increased mental and psychological stimulation.

Mechanical apparatus will substitute our limited physical range (mechs).

THE D1G1TAL AGE

When we cross the digital threshold of life and finally digitize human consciousness – we will obtain potential immortality.

The Bio-Mechanical lifestyle will be a thing of the past.

Our mechanical prowess will evolve with the new A.I. species to a point where human consciousness can be downloaded in its entirety into a clone, with the ability to engage or disengage individual components (emotion system, visual system, sexual system, etc) for targeted experiences and the option to include or truly omit

memories.

Homosexuality is the wave of the digital distant future, possibly with multiple partners (tens, hundreds, thousands and millions – all at the same time), seeing as sex is no longer physical, necessary or desired – sex as we know it is an archived packet in a memory bank, accessible at will for a targeted experience or vacation.

Vacations will include downloading a defined 'consciousness understanding' into a personalized clone created in labs (hatcheries) all over.

Experiences through these "clone vacations" will be recordable in every aspect and uploaded after the "vacation" is over.

Length of time in the host clone varies.

Although there is the ability to emulate experiences in a "Virtual Reality" program, it will become a necessity at times for self-preservation or evolution, to manifest in the physical world – in turn, clones can serve as vehicles for physical tasks as can remotely controlled objects (aircraft, missiles, spacecraft, mechanical, bio-mech, etc).

All of space-time is finally mapped out, just as the Human Genome project mapped our DNA.

All stars, lifeforms, cultures, planets, universes, black holes

– all known, all understood.

The space-time mapping will be available to all, instantaneously, as unlimited amounts of information can be streamed with the level of connectivity we will have achieved – the unlimited encyclopedia/dictionary/phone book/archives of life.

Parallel universes become an explorative purpose, leading the next evolution – hoping to stumble into a more advanced parallel world to learn from and take information back.

Would it be possible to track the parallel universes or dial in on the ones that do not match the same evolutionary pattern as ours?

Through trial and error (or possibly through harmonics and mathematics) it could be ascertained which parallel universes were more advanced (and by how much) as well as which are more primitive (harmonic vs dissonant)?

Should it be our social responsibility at that point to assist these less advanced parallels with the knowledge they need to advance to our current state of understanding?

If so, would that synchronicity drive the next evolution for our computerized species or just speed us along on our way to the next step...?

Hold on...

...we can't even imagine a future like this at the moment, we are misled and guided off course.

There's only one way to get there; through knowledge and information sharing.

Educate yourself.

Stop dreaming.

Learn something.

Do something.

Chapter 99

(COD(EX)*pand your mind*)

Ica Stones

Atlantis

Sumerian

Babylonian

Sirius A, B and C

Loose Change

MK Ultra

The Northwoods Document

ChemTrails

Nasca Lines

Economic Hitmen

Carnac

The Philadelphia Experiment

Fluoridation of water

Long Count Calendar

Willie Lynch

Flower of Life

Zeitgeist

Zechariah Sitchin

Piri Reis Map

Thoth

Anunakki

Giza Complex

Fibonacci

The Bible Code

Cloud Seeding

Earth's Forbidden Secrets (Maxwell Igan)

Nibiru

Book of the Dead

Operation Red Sky

Operation Clover Leaf

Operation Rain Dance

Bohemian Grove

Quetzalcoatl

Cloward and Piven

The Emerald Tablets

Platonic Solids

Mer-Ka-Ba

Vymaanika-Shaastra

Kemetic Science

Lemuria
World Grid Theory

Percy Fawcett

The Crystal Skulls

WikiLeaks

Bilderberg Group

Vimana

Golden Ratio

Pythagoras

Machu Picchu

Robert Wuhl – Assume The Position

Kundalini

Freemasons

Prana

Zero Point

Sacred Geometry

Metatron's Cube

HAARP

Dogon tribe

Pineal Gland

Akashic Record

Scalar Weaponry

Information is power.

As we live within their confines, only information can create the transparency we need in our government, academia, and social institutions.

Smile (while you stick the knife in)

information will make us transparent information will make us transparent

will make us transparent information will make us transparent information will make us transparent
information will make us transparent information will make us transparent information will make us
transparent information will make us transparent information will make us transparent information
will make us transparent information will make us transparent information will make us transparent
information will make us transparent information will make us transparent information will make us
transparent information will make us transparent information will make us transparent information
will make us transparent information will make us transparent information will make us transparent
information will make us transparent information will make us transparent information will make us
transparent information will make us transparent information will make us transparent information
will make us transparent information will make us transparent information will make us transparent
information will make us transparent information will make us transparent information will make us
transparent information will make us transparent information will make us transparent information
will make us transparent information will make us transparent information will make us transparent
information will make us transparent information will make us transparent information will make us
transparent information will make us transparent information will make us transparent information
will make us transparent information will make us transparent information will make us transparent
information will make us transparent information will make us transparent information will make us
transparent information will make us transparent information will make us transparent information
will make us transparent information will make us transparent information will make us transparent
information will make us transparent information will make us transparent information will make us
transparent information will make us transparent information will make us transparent information
will make us transparent information will make us transparent information will make us transparent
information will make us transparent information will make us transparent information will make us
transparent information will make us transparent information will make us transparent information
will make us transparent information will make us transparent information will make us transparent
information will make us transparent information will make us transparent information will make us
transparent information will make us transparent information will make us transparent information
will make us transparent information will make us transparent information will make us transparent
information will make us transparent information will make us transparent information will make us
transparent information will make us transparent information will make us transparent information
will make us transparent information will make us transparent information will make us transparent
information will make us transparent information will make us transparent information will make us
transparent information will make us transparent information will make us transparent information
will make us transparent information will make us transparent information will make us transparent
information will make us transparent information will make us transparent information will make us
transparent information will make us transparent information will make us transparent information
will make us transparent information will make us transparent information will make us transparent
information will make us transparent information will make us transparent information will make us
transparent information will make us transparent information will make us transparent information
will make us transparent information will make us transparent information will make us transparent
information will make us transparent information will make us transparent information will make us
transparent information will make us transparent information will make us transparent information
will make us transparent information will make us transparent information will make us transparent
information will make us transparent information will make us transparent information will make us
transparent information will make us transparent information will make us transparent information
will make us transparent information will make us transparent information will make us transparent
information will make us transparent information will make us transparent information will make us
transparent information will make us transparent information will make us transparent information
will make us transparent information will make us transparent information will make us transparent
information will make us transparent information will make us transparent information will make us

Smile (while you stick the knife in)

transparent information will make us transparent information will make us

transparent information will make us transparent

Smile (while you stick the knife in)